The World Abandoned by Numbers

Michael Gregory

Owl Creek Press
1620 N. 45th St.
Seattle WA 98103

ACKNOWLEDGMENTS

Grateful acknowledgment is given to the following publications where some of these poems first appeared:

ANOTHER CHICAGO MAGAZINE: Gun
ARNAZELLA: The Lost Field
BARNWOOD: The Last Days
BUMBERSHOOT ANTHOLOGY: Each Time You Catch Me Like This
CALLIOPE: Lavender Woman, For My Son
THE CAPE ROCK: Mole Hunting, The Shield
CRAB CREEK REVIEW: White Limousine, Turning Calypso: Two
CRAZYHORSE: Examination
ELECTRUM MAGAZINE: Factoring In, Crows
INTRO 16: Shorelines
PASSAGES NORTH: Lottery
POET'S GALLERY: Elegy, After the Rendezvous, Halloween
TELESCOPE: The Body Becomes a Thing
TOUCHSTONE: Laundromat
WESTERN HUMANITIES REVIEW: The Border of Visible Light
WRITTEN ARTS: The Dead, Friar Lawrence, The Scaffolding
Z MISCELLANEOUS: The World Abandoned By Numbers

"Lottery" was also selected to appear in *The Anthology of Magazine Verse and Yearbook of American Poetry.*

INTRO 16 was published by THE DENVER QUARTERLY.

I would like to thank my friends for their encouragement and support.

Supported in part by the King County Arts Commission

copyright © 1992 Michael Gregory

CONTENTS

Symptoms of Radical Amnesia

Liturgy	9
Mole Hunting	10
Lavender Woman	12
White Limousine	13
Laundromat	14
Lottery	16
Gun	17
The Lost Field	19
Shorelines	21
The Hanging	23
Not Surfing with Robert	27
Crows	29
Elegy	30
Each Time You Catch Me Like This	33
A Meditation on Form	34
History	36
Symptoms of Radical Amnesia	37

Poems in the Tall Grass

Cumulus on Blue Mirror	41
Free Enterprise	42
The Shield	43
Living to See	44
The Universe Is Not a Failure	45
Turning Calypso: One	46
Turning Calypso: Two	47
Turning Calypso: Three	48
Love Poem	49
Love Poem	50
Love Poem	51
After the Rendezvous	52
For My Son: On Desire	53

The Border of Visible Light

The Last Days	57
Daffodils	60
The World Abandoned by Numbers	62
John on Patmos	64
Examination	67
The Scaffolding	68
Friar Lawrence	69
The Dead	71
Philosophy	73
The House I Love	74
The Body Becomes a Thing	75
Kite. Bluff. Voices.	76
The World Abandoned by Numbers (Reprieve)	77
Halloween	80
Red Barn	82
The First Cuckoo of Spring	83
Factoring In	84
The Border of Visible Light	86

Notes on the Poems   88

For Mary, Aaron, Elizabeth

SYMPTOMS OF RADICAL AMNESIA

he had imagined the first mistake
all the humans are coming toward him with numbers

--W. S. Merwin, "Kanaloa"

LITURGY

A gothic morning: chilled, wet fog,
The jagged teeth of city skyline
Invisible among the awesome clouds.
Spruce trunks, black as burnt match sticks,
Whorl their green smoke in the gray, and my
Poor avenue could be slate scree
Fanned down an evil mountain where I shiver,
Penitent, at the bus stop. A soul's integrity
Broken. There's this silence.
From a distance some unknown something,
A darker blur moving in the blur,
Is four paws, now, ticking into view.
The hind ones are white. They cross and uncross
Like frail drops of light until the dog
Is clear. Then, hedges, walks, houses
Refocus to a neighborhood just visible.
There's this pocket of no fog.
A gap. A black labrador loping is
The only music. Its head sways. Its eyes
Look at me -- a range of shadows in shapes
Meaning: Human. Not moving. No
Immediate threat. And I watch it scout elm leaves,
Rhododendrons, sniff one attraction
And another. That lost glove by the curb
In its stricken pose for weeks the brief
Clouds of the dog's breath over it.
An unidentifiable scrap halts her
On the crosswalk -- Cars fizz by, their
Two white canes stretched in front,
Headlights turned liquid, porous, atomizing
Into 6 a.m. like a last dream, waking up.
Oh, nothing sparks this stillness, no
Eee of tires cold like glacier melt
Over skin. The dog lifts up her eyes,
Wags off to the known and the unknown.
A show of strength from houses broad as boulders
Vaulting uphill, stepping stones to fear's cave,
I ignore. When the fog seals shut again,
My bus lurching through intersections,
And downtown's toothy grin begins
To drool, I know today I will not be crushed,
Or seared by flame, or shaken mad.

MOLE HUNTING

My neighbor feels chosen by God.

A beer in one hand, flashlight in the other,
We lapse from our suburban backyard talk
And lean forward on lawn chairs, the evening susurrant,
A few stars drilling towards us through the dark.

-- Something we thought we heard,
But our lights find nothing, grass, for a moment,
Restored to its green, and heaved up wandering tunnels
Or ugly brown mounds that have pock-marked
His years of lawn fanaticism. No other neighbor

Has been so blessed. Shit, why me? he says.

We slouch back, waiting again, almost useless
Eyes checking hose lines that snake into mole hills,
The water sounding illusory, a dream of water
That seeps through night like voices

Circling in drunken whispers.
He's tried it all: poisoned earthworms, snares
And traps. And now it's flood. His handgun
Ready when this most primitive of mammals
Bobs up, sputtering from its old knowledge.

*

The domed basilica of Saint Sebastian,
On the *Via Appia* near Rome, vaults like crystallized breath
Above passageways said to have once provided

A resting place for the bodies of Saints Peter and Paul.
The early Christian catacombs were galleries
Of the martyred, corridors of paintings and inscriptions

That chronicled, in shadow, the piety and beliefs.
Corpses of the persecuted tiered into the walls.
A few bones and dust now. Memories. Pale

Candles. Reverberating voices. Like incense
They return, the martyrs, so I can stop them, ask
Why did you hurry to the prisons, the *Colosseum*

With its wild beasts? But no one can say exactly why
They spit on Rome's crumbling statues for just another
Mystery cult, a dead Jew barely understood.

For reality beyond knowledge? Hope beyond the grave?
Those unbelievable miles of tunnels a large-scale
Scrawl, an illegible record, even from an airplane.

*

We talk farther in the dark, another beer.
A mole does not fear the separateness which makes a human
Face more tender. It claws a space for breathing, drops
Into shadow, keeps a different, a difficult sense

Of itself to itself. The evening tips its dark fedora
And spills the spinning stars like jewels. Is our world
So evil? The wind, with juniper on its breath?
The mole's success is digging, and never the golden vein.

My neighbor's giving up on moles tonight, and we
Don't care, being drunk. Feel good, in fact, released
From our vigil, our blind brother and his gurgling
Caverns. Where did all that water go, that other

Voice speaking for us? Its message, *Take this
Fear away*, was crude and garbled going down.
We listened, part of a night, to translate his response.
The scruffed-up children, playing late,

Scream like whistles. A mole's face is on the moon.
In separate dreams we'll strain and sweat,
To get our tunnels perfect.

LAVENDER WOMAN

She keeps her pills with kitchen
Herbs and spices, in a cabinet near
The pantry where potatoes stretch
Dumb roots, tunnel weeks in air full
Of less. She keeps her knives sharp,
In rooms like holy lands
-- the 1930's couch, the chestnut clock.
Better spit out your Nietzsche in
That brass waste can. This year
Harvest was abundant behind stone
Garden walls, bouquets of red
Violet rising like faces in fog.
Old London. A voice would cry out
    'Who will buy my sweet lavender?'
And people would appear in rough doorways.
Lavender made into wine, crushed
In the sugar, or floating on a steamy
Bath, her hair that arcs and rolls,
Ravens in flight. Mrs. Santolina
Curves like light around these noonday
Crowds, their voices strike the wind
And burn, their conversations
Buzz her ears like flies.
    'The world is power and nothing else'
For those of strong will, to whom the true
Virtues are cruelty, cunning, hardness.
    Etcetera.
Her dress wraps her up in question marks.
So, where does she go, with the leaves
Dancing death, her walks announced
By flowers on that old blue nurse's hat.
Maybe bread on sale at the deli. Maybe
She collapses at the foot of a cross.
At night, the wind exports sweet lavender
And her footsteps drop across the lawn
Like candle wax. She has her life.
No one can trespass twice.

WHITE LIMOUSINE

From the old French, *limousin,* meaning
Coarse woolen cloak, meaning translation
Of the bottom line in your lizard-brain
Dreams of protection against common morning,
Common night. Gene, father, you go too far.

It has that startling quality of sun.
Or, nearly silken in those scrubbed
Twilight hours, sits and glows,
An affirmation. It knows what humans
Are made for. Climb inside: a human mouth.

Afternoons, you at the round cane table
With slices of melon, the reflection
Of light blinds statues in the garden.
Each clipped tree, shrub, or stretch of lawn,
Waves in the faint whir of that circuitry.

Your reflection, on the province of hood,
Is a new penny dropping through a white lake.
A last sip of coffee and you are swept
To a blue-green pool, blue-green games,
Blue-green ocean where your boat lolls.

Women in linen sink into shadow.
Men in pastels duck through the door frames
And your chauffeur accelerates
To the needle line between thrilling
And dangerous. Ice twirls in the drinks.

Near the ruined brick, reckless music, it's a slow
White leopard transcending streets,
Something that breaks our vision a moment
And is gone to its immaculate pursuits.
As they say, Gene, *a grand frais*, at great expense.

LAUNDROMAT

Last week I floated through
The buzzed glow of a video arcade,
Half curious, half dismayed
With the odd feel those screens project,
The silence of certain players.
They twisted knobs, yanked levers
To transistorized limits but there
Weren't enough quarters to light
Anyone's eyes. Here, my quarters
Know the rules, go down slots expecting
Nothing more than to bring
These jeans and socks full cycle,
To the beginning again, first steps.
Coins pile up and wait in dark
Collection bins. And it's warm beside
The dryers. Sunlight left for China
The way some lovers leave, silent,
Blazing. The clothes soar around
And around. Get to where I'll
Claim them and go. Some kids are all over
The floor, playing whatever their
Mom allows. She relaxes those legs of hers
With a swish of pantyhose.
   Your dryer's quit
She might say, or smile up from a magazine
With
  Terrible about Africa these days.
From the look of things I seem to be
Tailing a lone fly as it drones
In circles, window to steamy window,
Confused why the air suddenly stops
In mid-flight. Going on. We wing it
Around the Kleen-Kings, those humming
Altars. Their portholes give us
A glimpse of the mysteries of normal
Wash/hot water. Usually, this place

Is a deserted monument
To bleach and honest enterprise
This late Sundays. The walls bare.
The chairs, immovable. No more human odor
To fog the clear flourescent landscape.
Most of the time, nothing happens.

LOTTERY

for Naomi Shihab Nye

Because she seemed interested,
And her dark felt hat was tilted back
Like a confident wager,
I was trying to get across
To this Central American
Woman how our North American system
Of gambling works:
Pick-The-Right-Numbers-And-Be-A-Millionaire.
It's just blind chance, I was telling her.
I said it's the luck of the draw.

Oh, she said, in a kind Spanish
That picked through empty pockets, like when
Some soldiers come suddenly at night
Whose hands have been blackened
From curling up in the darkness,
Their eyes red from weaving through jungles
Where reality has become . . . well, altered,
Overruled, and the first who hears them
Wakens, cries out slightly,
Stirs their attention
So they turn to that hut first
And throw open the shaky door --
But there stand the welcome soldiers
Her whole village had waited for, and knows,
So this person sighs,
Offers the one with the worst uniform
A drink, a cigarette, some talk, whispers
Buena Suerte, hums her child back to sleep.

Yeah, I said, it's just like that.

GUN

The other day I went to buy a gun,
One of those seven shot Colts
With the sandblasted walnut grip
& satin nickel finish. It weighed as much
As a medium-sized soup can.
Near the glass display I took sight
Finding the dark, heart-shaped center.
Everyone in the aisle went stupid-mouthed
Or ducked as I leaned into a squat,
Stiffened both arms out, both hands
Welded to a steady, objective truth.
A sense of humor is a real necessity
Living in America. It could have been
Anyone.

        People on the bottom line
Often wear this vague, unfounded smile.
Like the poor in Arkansas. Maybe
Suffering is a kind of satisfaction.
I've read that before someone is born
Their spirit chooses time, place & circumstance
For the best path back towards God.
We pick our lives for lessons to learn.
A starving newborn on the Sudan plains
& a baby Dupont both suffer & celebrate
To one end. The derelict, the lifelong
Loving friendship, will wear one crown.
Because

        of your desire, you are deceived.
Because you are deceived, you desire.
Before you figure it all out, you die.
But I only add that since I'm cynical
& poor, & it was a perfect day
In mid-September when the manager made
Me leave, unloaded gun or no, leave
The trumpets, cameras, stereos, luggage, watches,

Picture frames, rings, TVs,
Leave all the pawned ambitions red-tagged,
Reflecting bare fluorescents, my smile briefly
Across the microwave glass before I hit
The pavement again, let my life bleed
Like Sebastian pierced with arrows.
The poor can smile too. When we wake
From dreams, hair-trigger, the gun in our mind
Is not a gun in our hand. The usual sun
Flares up, or not, a kind of cheap enlightenment.

THE LOST FIELD

Atop his red Harvester, your father
Sees hillsides trampled by the wind.
Guns the diesel and stops. That vast
Green blanket ripples beside him,
The tractor prow of hot tin bucking in it
As his only important star, our sun,
Dissolves in the black mouth of storm.
You watch from a plain house, from
A fence of cottonwoods guarding
The porch. In the kitchen, cookies
Steam up from mother's boredom,
Are laid down on the table with
Your story of grief, divorce.
Her hands are thinner; yours smooth
The oak grain absently in rough spots
Of conversation. Leather bags slump
In the clean scent of your old room,
A ticket in the bureau mirror-frame
Idles. You keep staring at her face,
Surprised at new lines crouched
There like guilt, the tied-back
Gray hair a rag over her shoulder. You're
About to say something with the word
'Berries' or 'relief' in it when the screen
Door slams, slams again down a hall
Of childhood -- the dark shed, the still
Meadow near the end of a path.
Slams like rain on the attic window
Where no one knew you hid. Father
Mumbles, kicks off his muddy boots,
Another day's luck, his words lost in
Wind crackling over fields, a voice
You remember hearing --
Crumbled furrows, their wildlife of insects;
Clouds, so massive, almost rumbling;
The skirt you made yourself, cut

Finger and all. A breeze against your legs
Kept returning you to pace
The dry corral. And you don't remember
Walking out, past the Frigidaire
Humming full, out past the place where
The wide swath of harvest stopped, the air
Loud, random; where pale stems
Struggled to put down feet, and underground,
Small waters seeping, rank roots, the dirt
Breathing its dark.

SHORELINES

At the bay, wind feeds me stray sand
And I pretend to enjoy the ocean. A cargo

Of drums and matchbooks stamped 'Philippines'
Washed in from a wreck

No one forecast. Matchbooks, useless,
Sag in wreaths of kelp, waves beach themselves

And bone-white drum skins. It isn't easy,
This dark face circled

In their shine, because the setting is
Lukewarm, and east, the first stars

Won't spin like mad. I tune to
A foreign language broadcast

And it's relaxing not to understand.
I try to fill up with nothing, listening to it.

But syllables I imagine are children who
Wear green, gray and black layers,

Or someone who dances
Possibly to drums. It can't be

Toys from a sweatshop that put my shoes
Up to their throats in surf. I heard

Rain on a woman's back,
Heard village huts crouch at twilight

In a country I can never remember
As real. There are times you decide

To stay living. Even rust is a kind of ripeness
For instruments bobbing on phosphor

And the foreign-looking stamps on matchbooks
Bleed beautifully. Soon, sunlight

Will flare up over the dunes,
Start the drum roll I'll march to

With my split lip and notched ear, with souvenirs
Picked from these tangled elements.

THE HANGING

for David Wojahn

I don't know much about railroads,
Or the iron logic connecting
Water, fire, a rumble through vague towns,
Except as a child that five-car Lionel
Ticking through living room countryside:
Its whistle on the coffee table (*a plateau*),
Twin silver arcs banking to a tunnel
Made by wall & couch, but this only
On certain days, like Christmas --
Neighbors over, ones I didn't even like &
    Quite a set-up you got here
While Mom swung her drink
    Sorry, no place to walk
In, what I'd call now, her Funny/Glamorous
Style. *Dad* was a word other kids used,
The period ending their scattered talk
Of garages & trips. It was a word
With an exclamation point sometimes
When my face mimicked Hurt, to gape an old wound
In my mother.

          Fathers for me involved railroads:
A bright bend in the forest that the steel
Followed, a voice hooing black corn at midnight,
Wind on its way to some place else.
It's how I've come to this photograph
By O. Winston Link, who focused everything
In his concentration on steam engines,
The Norfolk & Western, circa fifties.
This black & white hung here in the gallery:
Texture of flashed hillside, engine silhouetted
On a bank of its own cloud just exiting
A tunnel where father & son hold hands, the boy
Gripping the hook of a lantern (*a star*)
& the implied, onward movement
Of a train down a track.

                    That father and son
Seem unmindful of us, we who came to look
Beyond the eye level of looking. Either, or both,
Could pivot now to face us, but aren't thinking,
Frozen in that field. The train with its
Small moon searing one October night
Could merely pass the frame, & they would pass,
Glowing, over scrub & shale to a few lights
In some valley, wind, a house with
Tight-lipped logic, & sleep,
If I let them.

                    An uncle would okay my cousin & I
To hunt with him on Pennsylvania hills.
Pheasant, deer -- what the season licensed.
Maybe a squirrel or rabbit just to shoot.
He taught us the steady eye, the patient finger,
Ways to decide to set loose the moment.
I don't know what drove me there so often
Except the terror my body glowed with.
What I remember most
Are clean-glass Saturdays when, as children,
We managed to be quiet, following behind,
Each rustle or snap stopping us cold,
& we'd brush along until a radiant space
Opened where rail lines cut through,
Altering everything.

                    Our breath in cupped hands.
Platinum footprints in snow near
Crystal ditch water. The sense now that, staying,
That corridor of seeing would complete itself
In us, & we'd be teased from life.
A silence was there like a frozen globe
Hollow around us. I'd balance a while
On a rail, & then he would lead us
Through the dense woods.

Just last September
We walked the open-air market, my son & I
At the spice shops and fish stalls,
Hawkers shaking lobsters in our faces.
& I explained to this second grader
Something of art. Meaning, the Sankai Juku
Dancers could flex their bodies to choreography
He'd walk a bit farther for, that they'd
Gesture from a rooftop, ankles roped
For a dance hung in mid-air. Loudspeakers
Larger than a man filled the streets
With whale grunts, voices, trains,
& shrill electronics.
The sound of their instruction wrenched us.
A hanging, it was billed.
Tilting our heads back, we were
Two of a thousand people being quiet
In the vivid light of a lunch hour,
The last Yoshiuki Takada saw
Before his hemp line snapped & he simply
Dropped to the pavement.

The sound his body made, like Christmas
Ornaments packed in straw and dropped by
Drunken hands from a ladder, swept me
Reeling back to Finney Creek
--days and footsteps away.
The ice with its ticking noises
From cold air squeezing crystals tighter,
& the banks we walked still snowbound.
My son & I finished
The loop trail & our snacks in the blue
Palm of daylight, found animal prints
We couldn't name, wondered how time would pass
In the cabin we stopped to peek in.
No one home. Details through the frame
Of the porch window let us learn
The scruffed wooden furniture, beetle-green

Kerosene lamp, & the knickknacks
Of someone who was missing that day.
We saw a whole life we could know
& never explain to each other, staring
A long time & holding hands.

     If, when the moon finally touched fringes
Of treetops, we turned up our collars
Walking & thinking of almost nothing,
Then it might have been the same
For those noon crowds turning from that moment
As though wind swirled up from the place.

The student-of-philosophy-turned-dancer
Never moved. His body, smoothed by rice flour,
Never looked silly, or lessened, but had the posture
Of a child stretched out watching clouds.
An ambulance pulsed. The afternoon
Became a shell of air
Cupped around each of us, the bums & tourists
& traffic, a still life, a photograph
We watched as from a distance.
Walking, saying nothing,
Past a train station near the water,
I wondered if my son could feel
That intensity in the rails. Tempered steel.
Feel them vibrate as I used to,
Balanced & fearless
Away from the hunting, those bolting retreats
Animals made running. The same as they ran
When a long train rolled & cleared tracks
Like a father's warning: a shout
Sending birds falling up through the trees.

NOT SURFING WITH ROBERT

1972, Newport Beach, you marched across
The blond sand of our burnt-bright California
Gripping with your feet like the wrestler
You'd been in college, muscular Japanese body
Shining with oil. Me paced behind you, six months
From eastern brownstone, inhaling sea air
Like a drowned man come back. You drove us down,
Talking sorcery and shifting gears, to teach me
This: The Wedge, you called it. Rock dunes
Built for a jetty interfered with waves, drew
Out that old, malicious laughter of the sea,
Made a churning section for swimmers
Who strapped on fins, bodysurfed
A tempest in personal duels.

High tide salt air. More sailboats than I'd seen.
I was on one, harnessed in to windward,
The canvas taut as muscle, triangular,
Like a kite. Hot to swim, you reeled
Me back. I was dizzy, limp, said, *Not Yet*
As you strode to the ocean, looking back:
That Fu Manchu beard, demonic grin,
Black fins dangling from your fingers.
The sky stretched above boats burning the horizon,
Their names like Lucky Lady, Voodoo, Grandpa's
Toy. I said *Adios, pal,* when you couldn't hear me.

Outside the house I lived in as a child,
My father rolls a Blue Flame two-wheeler.
The chain link fences make safe track
Though my heart, like an urban, school yard window,
May shatter any second. Gripped under the seat,
His hand steadying me, pushing as I waver,
That sweat on my lips a familiar salt.
Look straight ahead, Keep pedaling, Steer!
And my face hurts in its stick smile, the far end

Of the school yard rolling beside me, is a slowly
Shrinking figure I can only glimpse
Without toppling over. His funny wave.
A half smile.

But that's just a daydream on warm sand.
My father, struggling lawyer, drank himself
Down to County Hospital before I knew
Who he was. Some after school sitter, who
Loved her new bra, who itched
To be with friends, guided me through
The yard, and I made my turn at the far end
Without thinking once of my father.

Robert, everywhere I turned my eyes
Was an unbroken pattern that day: cars swollen
To parking lot barriers glittered like a tide,
A spray of sunlight -- no, gulls!
Over the lip of a condo rooftop as I
Leaned forward to meet a sea breeze skipped
From the other East, the gulls confetti now, swirled above
Our heads. And you, on a strong kick, into the mad
Heart of the waves.

The waves slammed into rocks, the shore, themselves.
Cheers broke from onlookers as one or another
Ruddered himself through a patch of violent water.
No one hurt today. No bodies wrenched.
No one noticing the past --
A riptide that sucks us from now
-- how quickly one can drown. You knelt
On the blanket, water drying on your shoulders.
Collapsed, breathing hard, no words to say.
I picked up your dropped fins and stared,
Their glossy skin already starting to salt.

CROWS

Crows sound paradoxical
In the blue hum of desert.
Sometimes people forget that
& get gypped of a sense
Of their sympathy. Crows understand us.
They squeeze knuckled talons into fence posts,
Glide like ink to the roadsides to watch us,
& we zoom past in the shells
Of our dreams, one life shrunk to a dot,
Another, its circle yawning closer.

The crows hop down. They inspect.
Inches from earth the debris must look
Magnified, disproportionate -- each odd scrap,
Every lost part of motion, a giant wreck.
They pray for us. At twilight
I've risked abandonment, the highway
Loose in its heat underfoot, walked out to
Some arroyo that cracked open
With their voices & listened to them.
I let one shift a scorched eye
& summarize my life. His tongue
Licked the smiling corner of his mouth.

I would love night to fall like they do,
Strong wings, not black with evil,
Where they find me, another casualty,
Face up in an odd gesture, the malachite
Rocks humming with dusk's only voice.
They move in & aim their beaks
Until I'm picked clean, pronounced healed,
Bones dazzling.

ELEGY

for M, J & R

These friends of friends of mine stood
A long time braced on sheer granite

Far in a labyrinth called the Beartooths.
Clouds seethed over them. The hours

Swept by like spray off the bow of a ship.
This, after they'd buried their child's image

In a deep fold of canyon below, after
We'd hiked days with them, scuffing up

Switchbacks and leaning, moments, to icy
Green water, pure sound over golden stones.

Trailing this couple who said little
To their thin following, who kept

At the edge of campfires, our random stories,
The dim light dancing between their faces.

Days, those moody pantomimes of sky.
A league of private angels, wind-blown.

No one knew any destination. No one
Had to know that the instant an owl blinked

Into flight, through arms of evergreens,
Might have coincided with the instant

A small breath stopped in a small room.
Only that, by the end, their child

Belonged to each of us. As did the owl's
Smoke-gray silence just when you noticed it

Over a shoulder, and the blue-green openings
It careened through. The child, bone ash.

A tapered jar in one of their packs.
A silver, grim seed. They trusted

The clues they were given: a wave of a branch,
An odd constellation of mushroom caps.

Evenings were high meadows savoring sunset,
The veering barrenness of a slope

Of rock and ice. Sunk in the afterlight
As the blaze cooled, we watched

Fish feed in acrobatics, the pines drift
In darkened air, in their luminous dreams.

Our couple seemed like the wind, obsessed
With moving to the next place, the next,

Their whispers translations from another galaxy,
An unknown language sprouted by the moon.

From a damp sleeping bag they rose and gestured
And drifted away one morning, awake to

The prehistoric sounds a forest makes
As fog roves the slate scree.

They disappeared into the folds of mist
Like shadows sliding into shadows.

We ate breakfast with the sun's heat
Vaporing the grass, the lake rippling,

Altered by the wind's emotions, and flyfished
The day until their return --

Smiling now, hooking thumbs in each other's
Back pockets, they leaned together, described

The particular feelings granted to those
Who could stand and let the wind blow

All through the body, through the eyes,
At the edge of what remains:

A horizon which, for them, became a shoreline
Instead of a cliff, wind with a sound

Of ocean waves stepping back, leaving
A pattern sheened on sand. The light

And passing shadows making you blink.
The taste of salt in your mouth.

EACH TIME YOU CATCH ME LIKE THIS

A bum at the bus stop wants money.

It would be a leaf dropped from summer
Into his uprooted hands, their fingers
Twisted near my face.

My pale shirt passes like a ship's sail
Out of reach of his mad island,

Its red and yellow Shell Oil sign
Like a flame in the sunlight.

Under an awning later,
His face reappears on a glass storefront.
Its history of taking risks. A magic mirror.

In it, I push all the red chips
Center table with a smile, a belief
Behind my fat cigar. The bones of my knuckles
Roll like dice on the pavement.

For lack of a trump, my clothes smell acrid.
The neon partiers sidestep me like
Overturned garbage. But somehow

Our eyes can meet, we breathe so close,
Are put in opposite directions by
The moon's slow motion flip
Over skyline. I work your soul
On First Avenue, and sometimes
You walk away with the change.

A MEDITATION ON FORM

You can almost catch the *hey-ku-ee*,
The several redwing blackbirds, almost
  Imaginary . . . Charcoal dabs across that bare
Crooked branch. Their shoulders show us
Scarlet stripes like the two great wounds
Of our being, reason and desire.
  . . . but this, only before they drift to reeds,
(*The spare shadows of reeds floating*
On the glare of tides)
Keeping their cards close to their hearts,
Staying with a place of two waters
-- river and lake --
Where no one can easily walk.

Sometimes you've seen them scorn a farmer,
Peck at oats or wheat . . . though last year,
As usual, they unhooked from cattails,
(*A daughter found a feather*)
Ate pests that could have stripped the crops.

The birds must feel owed, in that case.
But people hate them. The farmers sit
Saturdays in cafes to watch the regular faces
Sift through dust on main street.
They watch little Ginny grow, and fill out
Her blue jeans. They study the sky
Like philosophers, knowing what thunders
Up there will happen, eventually, to them,
And each one hangs over his own
Bitter coffee, tugs down
The beak of a yellow PAG SEEDS cap.

Our blackbirds don't suffer like that.
They're likely to spend bone-cold evenings
In corn stubble downslope from a barn
The Sorensons built in three haul-ass days --
Though, even the cold . . . they still preen
Their wings. They live, these birds,

So Greek. The balance and harmony.
The deep proportion of their movements
Over marshes which seem entirely theirs.
They congregate, make judgments
About the sky. In this breezy womb
Are bold enough to startle a driver
Slunk down in his combine . . . who turns,
For reasons he won't find words for,
To see those hard yellow eyes
Burn and veer away beyond him.

HISTORY

Sometimes it's like this
Photograph of an owl

-- majestic, severe, white --

Who
    dined on a large rat
Who
    feasted on a dead soldier
Who
    has eaten his way
Into a forest floor
Under the nearly imperceptible
Wing beat of natural time.

All we have is the snap-shot.
An owl staring blankly from a frame.

SYMPTOMS OF RADICAL AMNESIA

A flaming limousine rolls smoothly into the tree.
Music from its radio crackles out like a candle
Whipped by a terrible storm.

Ten thousand miles away it's lunchtime downtown.
In the restaurant, with friends,
With mini-skirted waitresses
Arguing in the kitchen like modern parents,
The jackhammers and gear whine out front,
Looking for a meal, some quiet air, you

Notice the water's surface shudder in your glass.
It's like some dance of kindness, echo of ocean,
A voice from another place you can't quite make out.

At your car door in the shopping center lot
The shadow under the car is an awkward space
Inside you, wanting to be understood.
Its oil rainbows and tiny diamonds
Of glass, whatever they could mean to you,
Disappear like dreams in
Dark folds of your wallet.

It's the working overtime that never adds up to enough,
TV in a room that seems, each night, smaller, the darkness
Larger, stray thoughts like an aftertaste of coffee.

In the bathroom of a bar, you don't know
Whose face you're washing, or who the carefree
Bastards are having a few more beers,
A few more opinions. Memory blows toward you
From an open skylight, radiates from rooftops
Like a billboard under static-y neon

But slips away, yes, like a fever.
The world shines, exactly like a dream
Of the other world.

It bothers you, terrorists burning cars, exploding
Planes, kidnapping the headlines. It bothers you
To have lost your real name in backyard breezes,
Rotating doors, in sentences underlined in books
From which you've created the fiction
Of your life. That first world of seamless light
Disguised as money, dazzling toys, the whole
Hypnotic fraud. There are clues hovering
Over the sidewalks in the dust of construction.

The bad boys clunk their black boots.
Their program of gestures takes on elemental meaning.
And odd angels, windowshopping, become part
Of some process, the intent of the silence
Maintaining these moments in between
Where memory is permitted to speak. What have you

Forgotten, there, at the edge of a curb,
The ragged edge of what must have been a garden?
A voice, its light the blue sparks
Of an arc welder cutting steel,

A song to sustain you, a moment
Enough like this one, with satellites and stars
Appearing beyond the skyscrapers, roving
Headlights that will glare all night, the someone
You were once, we all were. It's whatever
The heart asks, whatever the light
Tries daily to remind you.

POEMS IN THE TALL GRASS

Give me one who loves and s/he will understand.
   -- Saint Augustine

CUMULUS ON BLUE MIRROR

July's green contours, this lush
hammock where a day reclines.

The sky, without judgment, burns
blue. Clouds metamorphize to

clouds equally unknowing.
We wear nothing but sunlight --

perfect summer clothes. And have
freely divested ourselves

of non-essentials: city,
car, fears, the weights of ego.

I sit up on heels and knees,
between your warm thighs, listen

with closed eyes to the wind, faint
as dead Persians sighing. And

a sound -- you, dancing, draped with
intricate golden jewelry.

The tall grass rustles like silk.
I hear echoes of tiny

doors that closed behind us as
we rocked further and further

within, to the point where the
known passes through, our bodies

at their best, flung out beyond
bodies to the flooded air.

We lay simple as two stones,
quiet, lucid, solid, polished.

FREE ENTERPRISE

The world has left us somewhere.
I've been climbing on your breath,

your tongue exploring my mouth
so slowly, lightly, our faces

glazed. You straddle my hips, our
hair tangled together there

like this thick underbrush coiled
on the forest floor, and we

lie motionless, kiss after
long kiss. It has gone away,

that daydream of gray skyline
standing sharp as glass, faces

of people twisting home, numb
from work, our faces with them,

and corporations flocking
at another poor carcass.

Clouds like suspended problems.
We have disappeared from the

streets of that hazy city.
The hours now all become

sacramental, our hands bless
each other, lazy and lewd,

our commerce elemental
acts, simple, sensuous and

moment by moment. We bank
our capital, warm, fragrant.

THE SHIELD

Looking over your shoulders
at thick leaves and evergreens,

past the soft light of your face
to absolute blue, and then

beyond that -- Instead, I let
my hands fit your skin, hot swerves

of your body, summer fruit.
We learn our new selves again,

teach what we are and are not
through recognition, embrace.

The earth is firm at my back.
The sun, carelessly diffused

in your hair as you bend down
watching me cup each breast to

my tongue. I'm in the small shade
you provide, and whatever

else is there. Sunlight tanning
what I cannot see of you,

wet jewels gathering your salt.
From what flames am I shielded?

Moment by moment we lie
spellbound, alive, forgetting.

We have made love, we have made
ourselves shining and endless.

Behind you the green summer
falls like dust on every branch.

LIVING TO SEE

There is nothing in the mind
but moonlight, black waves, cold wind

on the dunes. It's scenery
bathed with a ghostly music

and has uncertain edges,
darkness bordered by the dark.

It is a fraction of us.
There is only this event:

coming again and again
to our same few words, the ones

for judgment, fear, delusion.
But here, the green summer sea

crowds out our thoughts, we look up
watching as the sky's warm blue

intensifies, the sun shines
as if we were rays of one

fire, as if the real land is
made clear through our desire.

I return to your soft sex,
open, fragrant, wet -- curled hairs

like fringes of a meadow,
your pink cleft where my tongue

darts and laps, a mossy spring
flowing quietly. Something

is trembling at the blurred edge
of the mind, but we are light.

THE UNIVERSE IS NOT A FAILURE

At last it seems we make sense,
you and I, face to face, one

sense, one desire, one smoothness.
In the full-blown air we flaunt

ourselves like a blossomed branch,
my hands moving on your curves

as if fine tuning the voice
of your passion. Everything

keeps going elsewhere, they say:
the breeze, the day, continents,

a million stars we can't see,
this sheen of sweat on your skin

as the other world reveals --
our voices, our bodies, slow

in the grass, falling away.
I kiss your throat, closed eyelids.

Moist, quivering, mammalian,
our borders blur. What to do

but know that Mind must divide
where Heart swarms with completion.

We have the next sweet moment
because this moment must yield.

Then, the world dissolves, only
a transparency remains

where a strong light shines through us,
our lives, each other, this world.

TURNING CALYPSO

One: Calypso:
Sea nymph who detained Odysseus 7 years on her island

Nine days I paddled, drifted
on a raft of scraps picked from

the sea's calm music -- there was
nothing found of soldiers, friends

who broke Hyperion's heart,
and Zeus flung a thunderbolt.

In my dreams I studied maps
that burst into flame, the sea

froze around our ship and chewed
like quartz teeth, like the demons

who roared at each horizon.
Our souls shook. I thought your face

was Circe's, and I was dead.
Your first words, more embraces

than questions, and your laughter
at my red hair made sea-crows

garrulous. I'm three years here?
Each time our bodies touch, lock,

a new life peaks, a darkness
crashes. The old world continues,

out of reach. Stars burn and fall,
replace my brute soldier's speech.

Under your caress, this dream:
we gallop on Circe's horses

through the waves, the sun and moon
wash up on shore, our lost toys.

Two: Calypso:
A northern orchid

Your body is an orchid
into which a young monk dips

his fingers, dazzled. The last
silver of the last stars is

that wetness on his skin. Your
smile flourishes and fades like

a candle flame wavering
in its hot pool. God's love.

The scent of a riverbank.
Slow hiss of grass when sunlight's

gold edge slides. The joy of green
bristling the backs of your legs.

It's so quiet, river stones
listen. Whatever is left

of us thins to dreams under
intricate nets of branches.

The grain ripens, bends lower.
If there was a breeze, your skirt

would arc to an ivory cave.
When we woke up from our nap,

ravens were scattering from
an elm, wings painting shadows

across your skin. We have learned
to re-invent our bodies,

create our fluent, fluid selves,
our confident song sung loud.

Three: Calypso:
A style of music originating in the West Indies

In a season more than sun
or south wind, we make our own

shifting horizons of tan
and more tan. The afternoon

draped over palm trees, the light
asleep between your warm breasts.

The Aztecs offered living
hearts to keep the sun alive.

Their words described things in two's.
Pleasure was this: wind and heat.

Life is less dramatic here,
pleasure is also wind, heat,

but music turns the sun's wheel
in native duple meter --

heartbeat rhythms. These songs take
jabs at local fools but skin

stays intact, lifts from passion
by lyric, tropical rites.

What do we know of the sun?
I see you by the light you

are, the wonder arising
now in movement, blue and green

graces like waves of secret
shores, the hidden shining through

a human face, oceans of
possibility, dancing.

LOVE POEM

Today is a day
When things
Can happen.
These hands of rain
Hypnotize me,
Clouds
Are maps, their fresh
Domain captivates
My brute
Columbus.
When you are gone
My hands
Remain
Cupped around your
Absent body.
Your tawny
Nipples
Work like charms,
Amulets that
Hold off
Silky sirens.
The sea, at dawn,
Is gold
Turned liquid,
Waving.
The curved,
White,
Breeze-filled sails
Shrink
Toward the horizon
Without me.

LOVE POEM

Summer's
On the phone, clicking
Her emerald
And sapphire jewels,
Promising me everything
Long distance.
I steady the receiver
To hear
Salt spray,
Bird-screech,
The muffled crunch
Of nude feet on sand,
Wind
Braiding through
The fullness of palm fronds.
Summer quips
Suggestively
In Spanish,
Leaves my ear
Sunburnt
And sweaty.

LOVE POEM

For a moment,
All of the other islands
We could watch,
Shining across the sea,
And all of the foreign birds
Stretched out,
Shining under the sky,
The sand
Our backs kept from wandering,
Stayed as welcome as your kiss
That night
Crossing the icy park,
When the wind tangled my footsteps
Into a kind of dance,
And your smile,
Your smile flashed like the snow.

AFTER THE RENDEZVOUS

When we have grown up again
At light speed
Into nervous individuals,
After our attempt
To erase fear's borderlines
With friction and sweat,
We drift back under the static,
Under the day, breathing.
There are flared clouds
Stalled in the one mirror,
Our hearts beat counterpoint
To the hum of an idiot Frigidaire.
There is a world
As though through dark glasses
-- almost like the world.

And after we have let loose,
Tasted the sugar and salt,
Cast everything sacred into the fire,
Still those question marks appear
Like hallucinatory sparks
Seen after concussion,
Or sharp, little scythes
To harvest the golden fields.

It's a Sunday silent as 2 a.m. in
Those polished corridors
Of airports. Fear is
A judgment we make
Against ourselves, the stranger
Speaking of departures.
But each time we kiss
And the body understands,
Whenever a caress
Burns through bare skin,
Every moment that sparkles
Is a step taken
In return to the first truth,
To one another.

FOR MY SON: ON DESIRE

You think you did not make this world,
Its different shadows, the hours of a day
Conspiring like storybook forests

To hold you from your goals. The blackbirds line
The branches with a faith in darkness. We
Invent the air itself, unleash our spell

And fly currents the spell
Creates. Yes, a voice sails through the world
That each of us hears, singing of continents we

Crayon in, like grade school maps each day
Our stubby pencils outlined.
Those unknown deserts, steppes, the generous forests

Perfect a scale of notes we sing in forests
Inside. No witch, no spell
Unfastens us. That voice is ours, our line,

Our hook. It's always evening in this world,
You could say, the brute work of the day
Done, a meal enjoyed and, rising, we

Inspect the narrow road that lifts, like we
Will, toward the horizon, forests,
A town aurora. The light could rival day.

We're always a farm boy on that road, spell-
Bound, lucky, of the world.
The woman in silk. Her voice softens the lines

From squinting years into the sun, those lines
Of doubt, of hunger, shadows before us we
Wrongly assume *are* the world.

Wild birds of a forest,
Say; the stubborn broncos. A lingering spell
Of weather like heat lightning lasting days.

*This is how we live: the shapeless days
Become a world desire shapes, a line
Of crumbs in a forest, crumbled from that spell.*

THE BORDER OF VISIBLE LIGHT

It dances today, my heart, like a peacock, it dances.
    The woods vibrate with cicadas,
        Rain soaks leaves,
The river roars nearer and nearer the village, O wildly
It dances today, my heart, like a peacock it dances.

-- Rabindranath Tagore, "New Rain"

THE LAST DAYS

There's this guy who stands with me
    Most mornings at the bus stop. We face
The long aisle of 15th Avenue as it
    Stretches left and right, displays
Parked cars, houses, choked sewers, evergreens,

The first humans, jogging early enough
    For the least poisonous air of the day,
Or encased in humming, jellybean colored
    Metals, protection against the ordinary
New hour, its white knuckles, its already

Burned breath a slipstream they steer through.
    Behind us the park, our urban forest with its
Few wild animals -- a bird, a squirrel, a stray
    Maniac asleep on a bench. And thoughts no one
Has time for. When someone recalls walking there

They hear sounds of trees in a delirium
    Of ownership, see the sky in a puddle, oyster light
Dull on a watchband, and are afraid. He is
    My age, I think. Blond, thinning hair combed back,
A paunch. Wire-rim glasses frame pale eyes that

Would know when Lennon was more popular than Jesus,
    A mouth that could flare like lit magnesium
Into brief, brilliant laughter. He is not
    Dressed for success, as I pretend I am,
Though we both head downtown for day shifts with

A kind of horrible alertness you see from small
    Frightened creatures on *National Geographic.*
We alternate peering left, where our bus will loom.
    As if that could salve the raw air.
As if the high school group, waiting for their bus,

The chorus of wise guys knotted at its center
        Wearing post-punk, preppie or retro/new wave
  -- Whatever we'd look ridiculous in now --
    Didn't draw direct, simple lines leading
Into a resolution of sorts: the so little

We comprehended, the so little we can impart.
        Maybe all we accomplished from the Sixties
    Was to legitimize blue jeans and self-regard.
        At our best, we believed in the power of spirit
Over the power of money, we believed something

Could be done about the derelicts and the smug
        Briefcases, the I-beams continuously riveted
    Into place, cities of graves, stone fences,
        Boat loads and plane loads of weaponry, the boredom
Of compact mirrors, lawn mowers, checks, matinees.

My bus stop friend begins to remind me of Schopenhauer
        And the foolishness of trusting either
    Perception or rationality for the truth.
        I can see that well-debauched old mystic
Ignoring his luminous clock dial, tugging on

Sneakers at mid-morning to walk, fingertip
        Wagging, blind to streets and citizens, to a usual
    Cafe for coffee. An argument with anyone. *Virtue*
        And holiness, he'd be mumbling, *do not come from*
Conceptualizing. We must break out of the prison

Of craving and ennui --
        Until the waitress shuts him up with a scone.
    My friend is staring at his feet now, the mat
        Of pine needles brown and soggy on our street.
Like exhaled prayers their green lives have

Floated to the stratosphere. In the last days
    Of that bittersweet time, when everyone believed
  In the words of a song or movement in a dance,
    When the news waves finally broke over our skin
Like little puffs of air, when the defects

Of intelligence were not clear, and domesticated
    Terror not real, before we dropped back into
  Safe, small towns or large, glittering corporations,
    When each of us, without knowing it, knew
That feelings were the truth, and intuition, genius --

In those last days we were still school children
    Rounded up on a bus. Heading someplace
  Not too different than we'd expected. Not certain
    That something was over, that we'd already
Passed by ourselves into the future. My friend and I

To these kids must seem the blur of adulthood.
    If they watch carefully, behind our odd dignity
  And out-of-it-ness, our faces absent-minded, they'll see
    Each step taken onto this morning's bus a reclamation
. . . *the charred feathers, smoldering flightbones . . . a twist*

Of singing flame rekindling . . .

DAFFODILS

The best way to look at them
Is to risk, lie stomach down on
Runty grass that's perhaps a little

Damp, facing them head on, hands
Layered instinctively under your
Chin. And, even better, is

To also imagine neighbors watching
From half-revealing windows
Glared opaque in morning light,

After they've stepped out
In pajamas, found the rolled Daily,
Backed slowly into shadow with

You on their minds. Then, you can
Allow your ribs to settle in
The flat, green, spiraled ribs

Of the lawn. Then you can be amazed.
From here, you're eye-to-eye
As their insistent yellow heads

Nod among each other, trumpets blared
In a pitch past hearing that
Announces your thin shadow to their

Hyperactive friends: ants, spiders,
Flies that zoom past
Like lost cartwheeling kites.

Some of the first up, their roots
Must tingle in earth's muscle as
Ice subsides, joints creak back

Into motion in the season's flex.
They're terrified of hands, fingers
Whose dual nature is to caress

And tear. So you calm them
With idleness, your rhythmic breathing
All they need to know of you.

Because, what to take away is not
A few days' glory, but enough
To squeak back up stairs, comb your hair,

Listen to the voice of catastrophe
In its same, anonymous radio drone,
Strap that watchband firmly

On your wrist, and go --

THE WORLD ABANDONED BY NUMBERS

Since Eden, we've perfected
Our falling. From birth we learn

Our stutter-step history
Disguised as swift advancement,

Always the taste of fallen
Fruit in our mouths, the stars

Hanging above us like fruit.
The cry, the shoulder, the sleep

Like drunkenness. We listen
To murmurs in a grave, sounds

Of faint whirs of circuitry,
A ghost in our evenings,

A spell. But something keeps watch
Over the meaning, without

Structure except between us.
The world won back from abstraction

Is already here: a wind
Which has circled the globe, our

Sighs, slow to other galaxies.
Incessant renewal in

The expression of hope is
Required. When we stare at

Sunset and wonder: is this
The back of the other world?

It was a moment ago,
The beginning of that world.

JOHN ON PATMOS

Ephesus is only seventy miles from here,
Not far with a good boat and two of God's graces:
Luminous sky over a calm Aegean.
I miss that city,
Berserk with everyone and everything
From anywhere you could name. I miss
Those shady pergolas at the wine shops, theaters,
Mule-drawn carts wobbling with baskets of harvested
Olives. The Temple of Diana, too,
I admit, but only its inspired, Ionian lines.
I miss my friends.

               Here, an island of rock,
Barren miles Prochurus and I have
Walked until we can tell when even a stone
Has been kicked out of place.
Yes, though I walk . . .

Donkey trails. Silence and wind. Silence.
Villagers take enough salt out of sea water
To nourish a few pomegranate, citrus and fig trees
But fresh water is scarce. There is
Time to think. Lately, -- is it the shimmering
Quality of this place? --
My mind is filled with
Raw music unlike the wind.

                       As we come to a river
We look for a bridge. I have looked for something
To burn up this distance between us, the fear
Flashed from Roman swords. The word of His mouth
Will be such a flame. I tell you,
I saw miracles at the Sea of Galilee,
In what was Jerusalem, the little nothing towns
And backward provinces, I tell you I was there.
My brother and I, the others, rough men
And ignorant, slow to learn

That the occurrence of miracles guarantees a world
In which miracles take place. The bridge, children,
Is our faith, here and now.

                  Yes,
I was born in Bethsaida. Knew nothing
But fish and the Law, thugs demanding taxes.
Tradition said everything would change.
I looked for signs. But what? Signs reflected
One to the other like a palace of mirrors.
The Baptist pointed Him out. I began to learn
Of transformation from a Master of change.
I stand now at the door and knock.
Time is running out.

                Already a hot day.
He is determined. We are all on the road
Following a small herd of black goats. Dust.
The people know Him, the five thousand
Fed, the convulsive young boy
Calmed. We don't know still what to expect.
We stray out of earshot and argue.
As messengers return from a Samaritan village
-- They don't want Him there? --
James and I explode: Do you want us to call
Down fire? One look.

Time is running out.
                I am an old man,
Who needs no pity. He loved me; I returned love.
Friends who met at some essential place.
But love always asks us to go on, go farther.

On Sunday last I was in the Spirit, alone near
The harbor, and heard a voice behind me
Loud as a trumpet. Turned. A squall boiled
Over the port of Skala as I watched

Lightning flash three times.
I couldn't think. The voice kept going
With words like a waterfall: meaningless.
Day and night, now, the voice never stops.
It follows me to bed and rises with me, it pursues
Me through the day in everything I do, my body
In a tempering heat like iron for a sword.

There is this world, and the world to come.

EXAMINATION

How long have you been a witch?

> My father rocked me, on a windy porch

Why did you become one?

> And all one summer a white rabbit's eyes
> Burned in my dreams, two red coals, or torches.

What demon did you choose for a lover?

> By seventeen, a loping motorcycle
> Had taught my vagrant legs to throb with one

What oath were you forced to render?

> Desire: Always take me further. Burn.

Where did you consummate?

> Then, much later, a barren plaza. I could come
> With my silver brush handle, but I turned,

What marks remain on your body?

> Caught my slack mouth in a mirror, my hair
> Sticky over my face. The weight. I owned

What injuries have you done?

> My father's jaw, my sister's midnight stare,

Who are the children on whom you cast a spell?

> And highways of ex-lovers' sweat and moans

How are you able to fly?

> Etched near my eyes. Nothing, but a hood
> Of wind, a green cathedral where I stood.

THE SCAFFOLDING

Before he could let even a brushstroke
Bleed into the mortar
Michaelangniolo Di Lodovico Buonarroti Simoni
Raised posts and cross-posts
For scaffolding under
The Sistine Chapel's vaulted ceiling.
Not to construct reality,
Since no physics can do that.
Or as if vision were constructible.
Birds whistled outside the clerestories
Throwing Neoplatonist echoes through
Columns of sunlight
And the dust, like ground marble
Or fog that leads to another world,
Revolving in the columns.

It took months of sweaty carpentry,
Fastening together
Amid cornices and pilasters
The coordinates to the supranatural.
Primarily a sculptor,
Knowing patterns of muscle, tendon, bone,
He did not commence his mural
Without the visible
Seen through to the invisible.
The light behind the light.
A way of ascent. The hardwood framework
Angled into the cirque of the Chapel
Like a preface, an incantation,
A belief that even the striving
Is beauty, is divine.

FRIAR LAWRENCE

At the end, I told them what and why.
Bowed my head for the ax. Nothing fell.

The Prince called me 'a holy man' and I
Was left alone by the bitter families

To pluck herbs, brew cures, and pray.
Another mortal, terrified soul commended

Into the hands of Christ Jesus, Our Lord.
A cold rain falls through a dozen bare

Birch and elms, a kyrie. Our cows
Chew all day in the field. Damp light.

A typical winter. How many have I counted
Since that night at the sepulcher? Children dead.

And me alive. I shook, I raced to my cell
To bolt my door against death. Each day after,

Whether in the village where men smoke pipes
Leaning from windows, or in the slated shade

Of forests drifting with vapors, peasants and carts
Out of earshot, looking for Solomon's red

Berries -- yes, I'd always expect them to show.
Turned suddenly to spruce trees, a wind,

The sound I thought I'd heard just angels now,
Laughing. For all my skill with nature, I cannot

Remedy this grief. Could not cure
The division between grace and rude will

Or keep those flowers, my charges, from the frost.
I thought I helped, but didn't help enough.

I should have pushed them both into the square,
Declared: Here, citizens, here is love --

And let everyone triumph in that light.
Not kept it hidden, like a scourge, or a sin.

Love has completeness no words and no embrace
Can match. If love is blind, it is not one lover

To the other, but the lovers to the world
Around them and to their own mortality.

I blessed those two with marriage in the Church
And cursed them with my fear, of Princes, and State.

If vice, by right action, can be made
Dignified, worthy, then this will be my grace.

Hold up this candle, friend, and know they're still
Alive: you can see them in my face.

THE DEAD

On the porch my child leans out
Catching raindrops on his tongue.
One thing about the living,
We are eager to accept simplicity.

Here is how they return to us,
In these drops, grains of dust
Arriving from unknown distances
Like the stars come all this way
Speechless out of death.
Those our forgetfulness have scattered
Flow down to where our bodies still walk.

Last week the archaeologists
Cracked open another tomb.
The cool air escaped past their sweaty faces.
Out of locked shadows the particles
Of a monarch lifted into the sky.

Crossing borders of visible
And invisible kingdoms, what the wind swirls
Mostly is not so special. Anyone someone
Knew. They pass through our senses
Like radio waves, like hours of a day,
The action of some imperceptible
Complexity that we could call grace.

So it is evening
And the rain beginning to fall.
Light like the inside of an oyster.

In the morning, in the morning
After a night walk letting rain glaze
Our cheeks, our heads tilted back
To swallow the drops and laugh,

When we awaken after the sound of rain
Has flooded our dreams, its syllables,
Its language of the other
Echoes in the room like the dripping
After rain. In the morning clouds
Have parted. We feel so much more alive
The world could be revealed.

PHILOSOPHY

Inside a chunk of ice
That split off from Reason
And currents carried to the shore

A child of the past was waiting.
Suspended in clear space
The naked figure glowed
With iridescent skin under copper skies
And a frozen storm of hair.

Sounds of townsfolk in houses
Came out to me as muffled waves
Across vacant evening sand
As I heaped my clothes on the ground.

The breath from my lips was warm.
The circle of my arms around the ice
Made small pools at our feet.
A harmless wind on route to the fields
Took all the other sounds away.

THE HOUSE I LOVE

The walls are on vacation.
I don't need them
To brace their shoulders together,
My own tough thugs
Who break the legs of the wind.

The roof? The gables flew off
To lie languid at a seashore.
Their cedar shingles ripple
Like cards I'd play
Gin Rummy with.

Intimate light that seeped
Through windows I
Pinched black without regrets,
& the dark ear of the basement
Is now soothed by daylight's

Warm voice, hardly noticed
By the punk who honed
His blade on my granite front step.
I remember his sour grin,
Engineer boots, breath

Whitening from his nostrils
Under the red & gold hands of trees.
This house I love smiles at me
From certain glass storefronts:
Wool coat, hat,

My list of secrets
Folded twice, stuffed down deep
In a pocket I double-check.
That kid I'll meet, we're brothers,
Boy Scouts being

Prepared. Both of us carry
Our address like a look, a tattoo,
A whisper blown into gloved palms
That we squeeze
& hold on to for warmth.

THE BODY BECOMES A THING

I know I was dark & young.

For blocks I had watched the sun
Sieved through clouds, or separated
Into strands of light
On the avenue. Leaves, the faces of passersby,
Glossed on windows. Each
Reflection sent spirit back
Changed into a kind of worthlessness
I let dissolve out of hand.
Everyone strode forward
In colors of the city.

A meter maid leaned through thin air
While salt blown in from the Sound
Made the edges of buildings soften & shimmer.

I know that the intersection
Was like a great unseen wall
That let us pool, slowly,
Into ourselves, stand numb next to traffic
& its banners of exhaust.
The sun was again a glint
Off a windshield, the dark-haired
Woman combing her hair, suburban
Punks in red shoes, all of us
In what seemed a moment before
A connection. Until
The tall lights released us
Swirling into other streets & shops &
Incommunicable lives, & my body became a thing,
A still point in this movement,
Strummed like a chord
Where I stood back alone,
Alone, & humming.

KITE. BLUFF. VOICES.

It could be made perfect by letting go
Completely. Wind would be its God.
The stunning blue sky, an *a bientot.*

Instead, with strong twine it's lashed
To my hand. The wind blows
And bends around the twine, singing.

Ego, it sings, ego. I reel
Out more line, the kite kicks
Upward, straining. It wiggles and bobs.

The air around my ears rushes
like a waterfall. I drown
In the blue-green afternoon.

And, coming stronger than that sound,
The giggles and shrieks of children.
Their voices raise the temperature.

On her way running past, a dark-haired
Girl scruffs to a stop and sways.
Smiling, I tilt my sunglasses up,

Only the sun is blinding, so
I really squint one eye
And smile. She moves her head left.

Half my face is squinting, see?
And half is smiling. I cannot feel
The twine slipping. The kite pulling away.

THE WORLD ABANDONED BY NUMBERS (REPRIEVE)

In this dream
I let what I know I am
Curve away from my sleeping,
A curl of smoke
From a watchfire, the body's coal
Deeper in beneficent
Night forest.
I call this joy,
Remembering. I lift
Through air, ceiling, prehension,
The heavy part of me
Sunk in darkness, my face
A gold coin by clock light.
But who needs money
When nothing
Is expected from the world?
No, there is nothing
Besides this joy.

*

The way mountains
Regard seas that have
Abandoned them,
Erosions, their rivers.
Abandoned,
The years of my life fall
Swiftly and soundlessly,
As all of the discarded leaves
Throughout history
That have rocked down in forests,
At night, with only
The pure high-pitched
Sound of the moon, no wind,
A few small animals moving.
When not propped up
 By numbers,

The years click away like
A domino run
Out to the frayed edges
Of the universe.
The years of my life flare up
Suddenly in my face, like the last
Minute of a moth.

*

Tell me again, Love,
About the numbers, how they link
And breed
Beneath the surfaces, there
With the inarticulate shadows of grubs
Who push and chew under scorched lawns,
Every trivialization,
Each hopelessness,
Crystallizing like molecules
Of false thought, how
They glimmer, coiling, hypnotic,
There in the store aisles which
Undulate with the self-possessed,
How we invented them
-- Out of nothing, out of the One --
To symbolize ourselves,
Our separation calculated
Ad infinitum. Tell me
If the numbers mean anything
Between, say, the two of us here,
With evening creeping in
Behind the flashing clouds,
Or across square miles of cities or
The coloring book borders of countries,
Green units of grasses
Or estimated mass of the earth,
Those sequential radio waves
That ricochet

Off galaxies like the click
Of billiard balls in a country bar
Where, outside, under the boot heel
Of a massive sun, the men and the women
Go on squirming.
Tell me again.

*

We have our faith in darkness,
In the rumbling shade
Cast by numbers as
We lay them up like bricks,
A wall to shut out ghosts.
They become
Our monuments, our large-scale
Tombstones
The seasons play over:
Leaves drop for the wind
And snow freezes in the cracks.
Where spring occurs in spite of them
And summer's heavy breathing
Blows across their long, gray lines
The way timelessness
Will blow across
When there are no more seasons.

HALLOWEEN

Every month of every year
The moon rolls clear of the clouds
To remind us.

And this is the last harvest.
Leaves rush into corners to sigh
And pile up, whispering prayers.
Today the everyday changes
From routine to ritual,
Things become more vague,
Closer to truth.
An unexpected breath at your shoulder
Is the wind gathering its spells.
Like frozen little moments of each life,
The sky collects swirling snowflakes,
To hypnotize us for that white sleep.

Houselights. Eyelevel stars.
The crackle of candles
In the carved-out pumpkins. Those
Floating faces startle, their shock value --
Is it seeing ourselves distorted
One porch after another?
Could these jack-o'-lanterns, as legends
Say, once have memorialized people
Who shared in the holiness of God?
A day to glory in all His saints?

They want to tell us
Everything they know:
The light, the burning, the movement
Past windows

Of children who, with shrieks and yelps,
Navigate the streets

With scant respect for the dead.
Animated, conversational,
They go to places imagined by the mind
So the mind can go there, go wild
For the simple handfuls, expectations

Filled by yet another
Open door.
All of the masks are a wonder, a horror,
The adults play-act fear and surprise.
The body itself, you see,
Is a mask, and behind it an eager child,
No one to fear
And worthy of love.

The mixture of voices stretches
Toward the sky, with its night frost
Lowering, lowering.
Each unintelligible
Syllable globed in a droplet
Taken swiftly from the present.
And left behind, in the soon quiet
Neighborhoods, a world transformed.
Like a fisherman's floating lights
Over the dark whirls and swells,
The burning remains, continues,
An ancient accomplishment.

RED BARN

When I come home now in the city,
As flat as thought,
It appears, an eclipse
Reversed, edging from the first
Summer-blown hills.
The ditches of its easternmost fields
Sway with iris. And mercy,
Like one sustained sentence
Spoken in a whisper,
Animates the cypress trees.
I have a single word in my mind.
Come forward, I will speak it to you.

And when windows alter
Into black mirrors, and my thoughts
Float away with soup steam,
It startles, a heartbeat
Of memory rising like dust
Trailed from a walk.
There are names, then, for the clouds,
The frames of moving shadows.
Like a voice I didn't know I heard
The rain came looking for me,
And made my familiar scenery
Shine the way rice fields
Must shine in Asia.

I was always spiraling out
Away from it, and winding back burned
By the throb of cricket voices,
Returned to the world
Of time, where all things end.
And when auto headlights
Inch across my walls, I know there are
Steps to be taken
That cannot be learned, cannot even
Be described. Grace, for instance,
Comes by plain acknowledgment,
Like joy caught in the throat --

THE FIRST CUCKOO OF SPRING

Cuckoo? Cuckoo?
You preen on a limb. High in the mind's sphere.
While your nestlings snuggle with a new mother.
Do you move through their lives
The way a soul sometimes flies
In and out of a body?
I'm carried by the wave of your subversive charm
-- the unseen, the other side of the moon,
Oh, "wild-in-the-air" --

You perched and sang when leaves lay scattered
As though a ledger mysteriously emptied
Itself of its debits and credits.
Cuckoo? Cuckoo.
You were there also when the snow swept in
As if blackboards filled with numbers
Had shaken them loose.
Near the swaying field
A line of equations freight-trained into a wall.
Only the sound of your voice after.
That's all.

Cuckoo. Cuckoo!
I keep on losing my memory. As though you
Do not live enchanted in one
Unbroken season. As though
You have no song to surround me
Like a chuckle. We are carried on
The wheel spinning so fast it looks motionless.
And I am finished, now, with stumbling, descent.
What I knew.
Cuckoo! Cuckoo!
Another day I go altered into.

FACTORING IN

The silver belt buckle of Clarke's tuxedo
Pants clicks rhythmically, around his ankles,
Against his black patent leather shoes. Marta's
Peach taffeta evening gown ruffles like so
Many sighs, thrown above her waist, a blossom.
A Mozart concerto is silly music
In the marble-floored dining hall left downstairs.
Clarke & Marta are physicists attending
An international conference in Old City,
Vienna, & met only tonight
At a long table of exquisite hor- d'oeuvres.
They make love in some dark
Hotel stateroom, the suite number of which they
Will never remember, even thinking back.

Somewhere in his mind, Clarke
Is aware that Bell's theorem is based on
Correlations between paired particles which
Are similar to the hypothetical
Pair in the Einstein-Podolsky-Rosen
Thought experiment, & that it might relate
To the way the *Schonbrunn's* intricate columns
Are spaced proportionally around the rim
Of that palace, contingent to the specific
Weight of the massive roof each has to carry,
& that the globes of its outside lights, shining
On the walls between those columns, let
Their yellow go liquid on the choppy dark
Of a fountain pool.

    Marta, in her backbrain,
Knows that once a photon is set in motion
The wave function associated with it
Would continue to develop according to
Schrodinger's causal law, until the photon
Interacts with the observing system, & that

It could correspond to the horse-drawn carriage
In the park called *Prater*, the way it appeared
To flicker, in twilight, as the hooves clopped past
Rows of trees, the couple inside not speaking
But staring out opposite windows,
Until the function collapses in on itself,
Loons bobbing on the Danube's surface.

Together, Clarke & Marta are beautiful
As two sides of an equation balancing
Each other, coefficient & cosine.
This poem, in commenting on the sweat
Of Clarke's brow, the blush drifting across
Marta's shoulder, could represent the cascade
Of numbers & symbols in the complex of factors of
Two scientists realizing they are
Falling over the edge of reason -- or the
Insignificance of any commentary
To alter the bittersweet workings of nature.
The moon from their window now slipping behind
High, baroque clouds, the mix of voices
& music & clicking crystal that might be
Returning to them as they resolve
Their theories on a huge bed, catching their breath,
Suddenly exhausted & human.

THE BORDER OF VISIBLE LIGHT

for Larry Levis

I am the angel you don't believe possible.
One foot is in the water. Behind us,
Where storm clouds or violent light should be,
Everything is deaf and dumb,
The moon keels vivid
Only on us, two figures pressed close
While I support you
So you can walk. One arm is an arc
Around your waist, one of yours
Numb at my shoulder, the reeds cracking
Underfoot. We've been slow to the river.

I am the duplicate appearing as another you.
So perfect, your fear, like a wound
In the soul, has become flawless.
Wind from the slightest movement
Of my wings passes over us.
When you look, you see them
As two flames
Of a terrible knowledge.
I keep my eyes down, watching
How your feet begin to forget themselves.
The bank is muddy. My free hand
Offers a thin white cup to your lips --
Leaving for you when to drink,
But before we are under the river.

I am the calm at the end and beginning
Of each of your acts, your shift of weight
Painfully slow, the resting up
For the next step. I do not know everything
About you, if your defeats were proper
And inevitable, if you were ground down
By life's lessons so that these
Flowers laureled in your hair
Are only an ironic tenderness --
I've made so many trips to the river.

I am not prepared to answer questions.
And, if you spoke, your voice would break
At astonishing news: that your bones
Want out, your skin begs
To sag off. Where we are going is both
Too far to imagine clearly
And keenly present. Actual. If fireflies
Were pulsing, or you could see yourself
As though through water,
Perhaps you could sense, not loss,
but a filling up. I am the trembling light
You will circle and circle, the last part
Of yourself left to believe,
The love separate from the body,
The swirling river.

NOTES ON THE POEMS

Mole Hunting: Recent mole eradication developments include explosives. By legend, Sebastian joined the Roman army to help fellow Christians. He advanced to captain in the Praetorian Guard before his faith was discovered and the Emperor Diocletian ordered his death. Usually pictured a young man shot with arrows, Sebastian survived the arrows, confronted Diocletian, and was then clubbed to death. He was buried in the catacombs, on the Appian Way, near where the Basilica of St. Sebastian now stands.

Lavender Woman: The character's name is take from *lavandula santolina,* a type of lavender flower. The quotes are from Nietzsche's *The Will to Power.*

The Hanging: *Sankai Juku* is a group of avant garde performance artists. They had just begun a piece in Seattle when a rope broke and one of the dancers fell to his death.

Elegy: The Beartooth Mountains are in Montana.

Each Time You Catch Me Like This is the title of a painting by Morris Graves.

Poems in the Tall Grass: The poems in couplets are in a form inspired by the Persian *ghazal* (from al-Ghazali, a Sufi mystic). There are thirteen couplets per poem and seven syllables per line. In Tantric texts, sexual orgasm and spiritual ecstasy are not distinguished, both are called *mahasukka* (great bliss), both are expressions of the same vital force.

The Last Days: The late John Lennon was criticized for his remark, "We're more popular than Jesus," made during a Beatles tour in Japan. Schopenhauer was a German philosopher. "Well-debauched" is probably fiction. He was influenced not only by Nietzsche and Freud, but studied Eastern mysticism, especially the Hindu scriptures. The ending words are from Denise Levertov's poem "Hunting the Phoenix."

John on Patmos: It is said that John, the disciple Jesus loved, wrote *Revelations* while exiled on Patmos during a persecution of Christians under Domitian. Prochurus is fictional.

Examination: The questions are taken from the book, *Witches*, edited by Erica Jong (H. A. Abrahms, 1981).

Friar Lawrence is a principal character in Shakespeare's *Romeo and Juliet*.

The Dead: The Anasazi were an ancient Indian people who inhabited the southwestern United States. Descendants are modern-day pueblo Indians such as the Hopi. One Anasazi prayer during periods of drought was for their dead to help them by returning as much needed rain.

Halloween: Originally called All Saints Day, a feast of Catholic and Anglican churches where God is glorified for all His saints. In medieval England it was called All Hallows, hence the name Halloween for the preceding day, Hallow's Eve.

The Border of Visible Light: The poem comes after Elihu Vedder's *The Cup of Death*, a neoclassic painting held by the National Gallery in Washington, D.C.